Think, Feel, Know, Enjoy

First published in 2016 by Brahma Kumaris Information Services Ltd,
Global Co-operation House, 65 Pound Lane, London, NW10 2HH

Print ISBN: 978-1-886872-82-0
Kindle: 978-1-886872-83-7
ePub978-1-886872-84-4

Dadi Janki's words, based on material provided by Juliette Polle
Compiled and edited by Donia Keith
Designed by Mike Saunders

Think
Feel
Know
Enjoy

Dadi Janki

Dadi Janki
Administrative Head
Brahma Kumaris

Foreword

Through the study of Raja Yoga we attain all knowledge from God, the Supreme Soul. However, do I remain in the stage of just listening to, reading or repeating points and of simply understanding them?
It is one thing to understand myself and what I have to do to fulfil my potential, but it is quite another to put it into practice, which means to experience it. Yet it is only when I experience something deep within, that the satisfaction comes of having attained something valuable.

I see it as important to give time to keep my mind concentrated and to experience deep, internal silence. I am able to remain introverted when I remain aware of its value. My experience of introversion is that it steers me clear of fluctuation or upset. Through the persistent practice of concentration combined with determination, my mind gradually reaches a stage of being constantly calm and still.

I no longer just take the support of God's words, but I understand the intention behind those words; that God is giving me the means to be forever peaceful and happy. Experience becomes my support, and God becomes my Companion.

Om shanti.
BK Janki

B. K. Janki

List of Contents

Do you remember
you are a spark of living energy?

A lack of constant peace and happiness is a sign that we have forgotten our true identity, and that we see ourselves as flesh and blood instead.

When we go deep beneath the skin, bone and tissue, at the centre of the forehead and between the eyes, the soul resides. The soul is the spark of energy that makes all bodily matter function; it is the spark of energy that enables the heart to beat and the lungs to breathe.

The energy of the soul is the vibrations of peace, love, happiness, truth, wisdom and bliss. Each action and interaction is filled with whatever virtues and qualities the soul desires to bring into play.

When the soul only engages in the purest qualities and highest virtues then all actions can be beneficial and good.

True life begins when we live in the awareness of being a soul. When we have accurate spiritual awareness in every moment, then soul consciousness becomes a natural way of life.

Realise that the soul is vital to life and to the quality of our living. Without it nothing can be experienced.

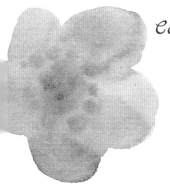

Consider for a moment that you are a spark of living energy.

. . .Think it, feel it, experience it, know it, enjoy it.

Do you remember you are a soul?

Remember you are a soul made up of the purest vibrations. The soul emits the vibrations of whatever virtue or quality it chooses to stabilise in. These vibrations include the energies of peace, love and happiness.

Positive qualities and virtues are the soul's innate energies. When we stay in the awareness of our true essence, the purest vibrations of the soul are experienced.

Let go of the awareness of your body and go deep into the awareness of the real you. Then emerge the experience of the virtue or pure quality on which you are focused.

The longer the focus and awareness is maintained, the longer the experience is enjoyed. The soul always maintains its qualities but whether we experience those vibrations depends on how well we remain in the experience of our inner pure qualities.

Consider for a moment that
you are a soul.

. . .Think it, feel it,
experience it,
know it, enjoy it.

Do you remember
the role of the soul?

It is the soul that brings life to its physical body; it is the battery, the energy provider, the life force. The soul is the means to enable body matter to move, to function and to experience life.

In every moment the soul creates, explores and expresses through the physical form within which it exists. Every action can be powerful through soul conscious awareness.

Consider the soul as a point of pure energy. It is eternal. It is indestructible. The soul stores data of everything seen, everything heard and everything experienced in all births.

The soul instinctively knows that when it engages its beautiful inner qualities and virtues, the experience of the moment is perfect. The atmosphere is charged with the power that comes from the soul.

Realise that the soul's role is to be powerful.

Consider for a moment your role.
. . .Think it, feel it,
experience it,
know it, enjoy it.

Do you remember your Eternal Father, the Supreme Soul?

Remembrance of the Eternal Father, the Supreme Soul, empowers the soul. Vibrations of peace, love and happiness flow into the soul and into the atmosphere from God, the Eternal Source of Pure Power.

Realise that when your thoughts are connected to the Eternal Father, there can only be harmony and peace.

God gives His own introduction, but the heart of each soul then has to recognise the Eternal Father. A moment of bonding occurs. When this happens, disarray becomes replaced with alignment, and our sense of depletion is replaced by fullness and strength.

The easy method to explore, experience and rebuild the power of the soul is to stay in spiritual connection with the Eternal Father, the Supreme Soul. The more the soul remembers its spiritual Father, the more the relationship grows, develops and deepens.

Remember that to the extent you remember the Supreme Father, the Supreme Father remembers you.

Consider for a moment your love-filled remembrance of the Supreme Soul.

. . .Think it, feel it,
experience it,
know it, enjoy it.

Do you remember
how it feels to be in the company of the Supreme Soul?

The Supreme Soul is eternally full of the purest energy and possesses all virtues and powers. In every moment, irrespective of where we are, we can spend it in the Supreme Soul's company and be merged in that vibration.

When we commune with God, the Supreme Soul, even for a moment, that moment is filled with love, joy and power. When two sparks of soul energy connect and rekindle their love for each other then so much pure love is experienced.

The more moments spent in God's company and vibration, the more our own vibration begins to alter and align to the same elevated quality. In this way God is able to show us our original pure and perfect nature.

The Supreme Soul always knows each and every soul better than we know ourselves, and by staying in His Company we can also come to know the Supreme Soul extremely well.

This relationship and connection with the Supreme Soul is personal and unique to every soul.

Remember that God, the Supreme Soul, as the Father of all, has endless love for all His children.

Consider for a moment your connection and relationship with the Supreme Soul.

. . .Think it, feel it, experience it, know it, enjoy it.

Do you remember your eternal home?

Do you remember your original eternal home beyond this physical universe? That spiritual, silent realm of powerful vibrations and pure energy?

The home of all souls is a place of eternal peace where the experience is always one of love, happiness, purity, truth and bliss. The atmosphere is the purest, the sweetest, and the loveliest.

In this non-physical realm, nothing disturbs the harmonious vibrations that each soul emits. Here, the soul resides as a point of light; a point of pure and powerful energy.

In the home of all souls, no communication is required. Neither are the roles, inter-relationships or positions of souls relevant in this realm of peace. Instead, souls are unified by a sense of one family and of all belonging to One.

Only the purest energies are emitted and exchanged in the spiritual realm. Here you are a bodiless being of light energy that radiates light in all directions.

Consider for a moment your eternal home.

. . .Think it, feel it, experience it, know it, enjoy it.

Do you remember to enjoy every moment of each day?

Each day is important and valuable. Realise that each passing moment is the most important moment.

Life is made up of millions of moments. The quality moments are those when the soul is focused, alert and in the present, yet very few moments are lived in this way and enjoyed to the full.

Moments that pass by without the soul taking active notice are not experienced as truly lived. When the soul realises that every moment is valuable and can be experienced as important, then time will be used and experienced in a worthwhile way.

Consider each moment in your day as the most important moment to be lived and experienced to the full. Realise that when you are mindful of every present moment you are able to express and experience the moment in pleasure and appreciation.

How much of your day do you experience and enjoy to the full?

Consider for a moment your enjoyment of your life.
. . .Think it, feel it, experience it, know it, enjoy it.

Do you remember
the art of experiencing?

The most important thing in life is to experience. To experience what?

It is the experience of being involved, like an actor in a play. The soul is the actor, the body is the costume, and all our activities and interactions make up our part in the play.

Each action is experienced by the soul. Realise that whatever action we perform, the seed of that action is a thought. We can choose what we experience by choosing what we think about.

Be aware it is always the soul who is the first to experience the energy of every thought.

To enjoy the purest vibrations and encounters, remain alert and aware in each moment. We should always stay in the present and experience the full strength of that moment.

Keep it in your awareness that once that moment passes, the opportunity to experience that moment is overtaken by the next moment. The opportunity to take benefit from the energy of the soul's vibration lies only in each present moment.

Consider for a moment how we create
our own experiences.
. . .Think it, feel it,
experience it,
know it, enjoy it.

Do you remember
your perfect form?

Do you remember the innermost part of you that is so perfect and true?

Time captures our complete and perfect form in a subtle region that lies beyond this physical world we know and live in. Yet we can travel to this pure and sacred place in moments. All we need is to visualise that perfect form of ourselves – our angelic form.

With the power of pure thoughts, the soul can travel faster than a rocket and reach a soundless pure world where only perfection exists. There, when we no longer deny our perfect form, we can look through a timeless mirror and see a beautiful reflection that resonates with the deep and long held secret of our authenticity.

Held in this angelic experience we are at our most powerful. Our natural vibrations of love and compassion flow effortlessly to souls crying out in this physical world below.

Now is the time to emerge your true and perfect form from depths long forgotten ... buried under the noise of this chaotic world, under the weight of responsibilities and the constant flow of fruitless thoughts.

Consider for a moment your perfect form.

. . .Think it, feel it, experience it, know it, enjoy it.

Do you remember
you are a powerful entity?

Do you remember that the soul has the power to change its thoughts in a second? By changing thoughts instantly, feelings can also change in that same second.

Do you experience how by changing our thoughts and feelings, attitudes then change? By changing thoughts, feelings and attitudes, observe how the atmosphere also changes.

The power of the soul is able to affect any situation, action or interaction instantly.

This is what it means to be a powerful soul.

Now is the time to fully realise the power of the soul and the influence this power has on physical matter, situations and the atmosphere. The vibrations we create through our experiences all spread outwards into the world.

Every soul can choose to emit the purest energy and vibrations into the world; just stay alert and only have the purest thoughts, words and actions.

Consider for a moment your powerful, positive influence.

. . .Think it, feel it, experience it, know it, enjoy it.

Do you remember
the use of the eyes?

The eyes are the windows of the soul. What does the soul see when it looks out through these windows? Does it see the best in each person, action and situation?

We see what we choose to see, and in every moment we can see the best in everything. We can choose only to see beauty; be it the beauty of the environment, the beauty within another soul, the beauty in a situation.

When our eyes only see the best in everything then all scenes in the drama of life are accepted and valued.

When the soul, which we can regard as the 'third eye', remembers to look beneath the skin of the body to the spark of energy controlling the body, then we can see the true beauty of others.

All souls seek to express their qualities and virtues as best they can.

In soul consciousness we see situations, people and occurrences through eyes filled with virtues and qualities, and our vision and attitude changes.

Consider for a moment how the soul uses the eyes.

. . .Think it, feel it, experience it, know it, enjoy it.

Do you remember the power of the eyes?

The eyes can speak without words. The vibration of the soul is emitted through the eyes. This is why a glance, a lingering look or a glare can be felt by others in a second.

Every look conveys something about us in terms of our attitudes, thoughts and feelings. Happiness, sadness, worry, irritation and anger can all be shared through the eyes.

It takes a second to step into the awareness of good wishes and a second to deliver those feelings through the eyes to others.

One second of peaceful loving thoughts conveyed through the eyes can enhance another soul's day.

Each loving look or glance can spread joy and uplift others through the powerful vibrations that are love.

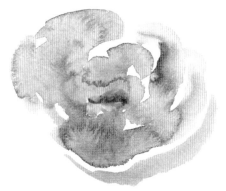

Consider for a moment the soul power of the eyes.

. . .Think it, feel it, experience it, know it, enjoy it.

Do you remember the spiritual laws?

Our lives are lived under the protection and support of spiritual laws that are absolute in their existence and execution.

Where there is law and order we do not need to channel energy into seeking justice or retribution, or to think about reward. We can keep our focus on that element of the laws which lies within our own control – the quality of own thoughts, words and actions in every moment.

Social laws or even physical laws are not unconditional – after all, one can create ways to defy gravity and to become weightless. Yet nothing we think, say or do can dodge the accuracy and inevitability of spiritual laws.

Truth will always prevail for example, and for every action there will always ultimately be a just return: in other words, 'what goes around, comes around'.

The assurance that comes from the spiritual laws should make us like constantly carefree emperors. Vigilant rulers of the 'kingdom' that is our mind and body, yet always remaining light and easy with what might be happening externally.

*Consider for a moment the
assurance of the spiritual laws.*

*. . .Think it, feel it,
experience it,
know it, enjoy it.*

Do you remember
you have a past?

As eternal beings, souls experience many actions, and have many adventures and interactions on the journey through many lives.

Deep within the memory tract, we hold the record of all our previous births. Like an internal DVD, all thoughts, words and actions are permanently recorded and stored. When 'déjà vu' is experienced it is the re-emergence of a moment that is pre-recorded within us.

When we accept we have a long journey and numerous interactions with many other souls, then we can understand why we may feel an instant reaction to someone, or to being in a place or situation apparently for the first time.

Spiritual laws cause our past to define what is to come. Simultaneously we create a past and also a future with each passing moment.

God assures us that whatever has happened in the past has been good, because within it there has been the opportunity for benefit. And that whatever is to come will be even better!

Consider for a moment the greatness of your past.

. . .Think it, feel it, experience it, know it, enjoy it.

Do you remember the importance of the present?

In each moment the choice of an experience lies within the soul. When we are aware that we make choices, then we can choose to have good experiences in each moment.

To attain the best experiences constantly, the soul stays in the awareness of its spiritual identity and which virtue, quality and good vibration it wishes to emerge in every moment. To achieve this, we remember that every thought and feeling we generate is a choice we make, irrespective of the circumstances or behaviours of others.

When we remember to engage with full awareness in every moment, then each moment can be sweetly entertaining. Every moment is both precious and valuable, because each moment can be shared in loving connection with God as our Companion.

The most successful moments are the present moments. The most powerful moments are the present moments. These are the moments when the soul can be conscious of itself as a powerful energy.

Consider for a moment the importance of this very moment.

. . .Think it, feel it, experience it, know it, enjoy it.

Do you remember your future?

As an eternal being, our future is also recorded within the memory tract of the soul. Consider that tomorrow already exists; tomorrow is already there waiting for the soul to arrive to be present in the moment.

All souls have their own part to play, and each one's part is different and unique. The only part the soul can play is his own; and like an actor in a recurring play, every moment to come is played identically to the time before.

When we understand that all is already arranged and exact, then there is no need to attempt to alter what is to be. There is the beautiful balance: to refrain from over-thinking or from applying force to situations, yet to honour every moment that is to come by giving it considered mindfulness as it arrives.

Because there is 'nothing new' in the scenes of the drama, then nothing need cause us concern. Each scene is original and unique and yet encountered before.

With this enlightened understanding we learn to live with attention, but never with tension.

Consider for a moment the greatness of your own future.

. . .Think it, feel it, experience it, know it, enjoy it.

Do you remember this time of awakening?

The actor can become so absorbed in his part that he can forget the overall story within the play.

This human world play in which all souls are cast can be known by several titles. It is the play of 'Day and Night', of 'Ascent and Descent', of 'Snakes and Ladders', of 'Ignorance and Knowledge', and of 'Victory and Defeat'.

Now is the time when we emerge from a night of darkness and discomfort, from a sense of stumbling around or of always being knocked back and unable to make meaningful progress, and from any feeling that success is short lived and will be pursued by failure.

At this moment in time we learn to shed our habit of body consciousness, like a butterfly that breaks free from its chrysalis. It is only now that we receive the gift of soul consciousness from the Supreme Soul; we awaken from the deep sleep of ignorance.

In soul consciousness we can ascend like the lark, and fly once more in those elevated realms of purity and truth.

Consider for a moment this special aspect in time.

. . .Think it, feel it, experience it, know it, enjoy it.

Do you remember
your place in this world?

Where do we each fit in this vast and multi-varied world filled with billions of souls?

The world has become like a big old tree: from its original trunk and main branches, many further branches, sub branches and twigs have sprouted and proliferated, each bearing many leaves.

Every soul of the world is like a leaf on that tree, positioned according to the fundamental beliefs and principles which it carries deep within.

We each share the need to find our individual and unique place on this human world tree. When we do find it, then the extraversion of our looking around and the need to search finishes.

Like how a star fixes its position in relation to all other stars in the sky. We become settled and stable like a lighthouse, and a means for other souls to navigate their own equally unique course. All we need do is radiate our light to the universe ... radiate our light ... radiate our light.

Consider for a moment your place in this world.

. . .Think it, feel it, experience it, know it, enjoy it.

Synopsis:
ways in which we become the embodiments of experience.

Experience your perfect, powerful form ...

Experience what it means to belong to the Eternal Father ...

Experience staying in God's company ...

Experience the eternal home ...

Experience how whatever you give to yourself you give to others, you give to the atmosphere, and you give to the entire world and beyond ...

Experience how whatever you do and whatever you give, there will always be the return ...

Experience the bigger picture; your eternal existence and your unique place in the human world tree ...

Use every moment in an elevated and worthwhile way; constantly serve and uplift the world through the silent word and the soundless chant that is soul consciousness ...

As often as you can, consider for a moment ...

. . .Think it, feel it,
experience it,
know it, enjoy it.

About the Brahma Kumaris

The Brahma Kumaris is a network of organisations in over 100 countries, with its spiritual headquarters in Mt Abu, India. The University works at all levels of society for positive change.

Acknowledging the intrinsic worth and goodness of the inner self, the University teaches a practical method of meditation that helps people to cultivate their inner strengths and values.

The University also offers courses and seminars in such topics as positive thinking, overcoming anger, stress relief and self-esteem, encouraging spirituality in daily life. This spiritual approach is also brought into healthcare, social work, education, prisons and other community settings.

The University's Academy in Mount Abu, Rajasthan, India, offers individuals from all backgrounds a variety of life-long learning opportunities to help them recognise their inherent qualities and abilities in order to make the most of their lives.

All courses and activities are offered free of charge.

for more information: www.brahmakumaris.org
for Brahma Kumaris publications: www.inspiredstillness.com

How and Where to Find Out More

SPIRITUAL HEADQUARTERS

PO Box No 2, Mount Abu 307501, Rajasthan, India

Tel: (+91) 2974 - 238261 to 68

Fax: (+91) 2974 - 238883

E-mail: abu@bkivv.org

INTERNATIONAL CO-ORDINATING OFFICE

Global Co-operation House,

65-69 Pound Lane, London, NW10 2HH, UK

Tel: (+44) 20 - 8727 - 3350

Fax: (+44) 20 - 8727 - 3351

E-mail: london@brahmakumaris.org